P9-CJM-360

On the cover:

Most **red foxes** are red in color, though some may be brown or black. Red foxes have very good eyesight, hearing, and sense of smell. In some children's stories, red foxes have been described as bold and sneaky. In real life, though, red foxes are shy and nervous by nature.

A Reading/Language Arts Program

Program Authors

Diane August
Donald R. Bear
Janice A. Dole
Jana Echevarria
Douglas Fisher
David Francis
Vicki Gibson
Jan E. Hasbrouck
Scott G. Paris
Timothy Shanahan
Josefina V. Tinajero

Macmillan/McGraw-Hill

Contributors

Time Magazine, Accelerated Reader

RFB&D
learning through listening

Students with print disabilities may be eligible to obtain an accessible, audio version of the pupil edition of this textbook. Please call Recording for the Blind & Dyslexic at 1-800-221-4792 for complete information.

B

The McGraw-Hill Companies

Macmillan/McGraw-Hill

Published by Macmillan/McGraw-Hill, of McGraw-Hill Education, a division of The McGraw-Hill Companies, Inc., Two Penn Plaza, New York, New York 10121.

Printed in the United States of America

ISBN: 978-0-02-202195-5/1, Bk. 6

MHID: 0-02-202195-7/1, Bk. 6

2 3 4 5 6 7 8 9 (027/055) 12 11 10 09

Welcome to California *Treasures*

Imagine having a pet dinosaur who wants to go to school, learning about how *real* animals act as teams, or reading about a kitten who thinks the moon is a bowl of milk. Your **Student Book** contains these and other award-winning fiction and nonfiction selections.

Treasures Meets California Standards

The instruction provided with each reading selection in your **Student Book** will ensure that you meet all the **California Reading/Language Arts Standards** for your grade. Throughout the book, special symbols (such as ✔) and codes (such as R 1.1.2) have been added to show where and how these standards are being met. They will help you know *what* you are learning and *why*.

What do these symbols mean?

- CA = Tested Standards in California
- ✔ = Skill or Strategy that will appear on your test
- R = Reading Standards
- W = Writing Standards
- LC = Language Conventions Standards
- LAS = Listening and Speaking Standards

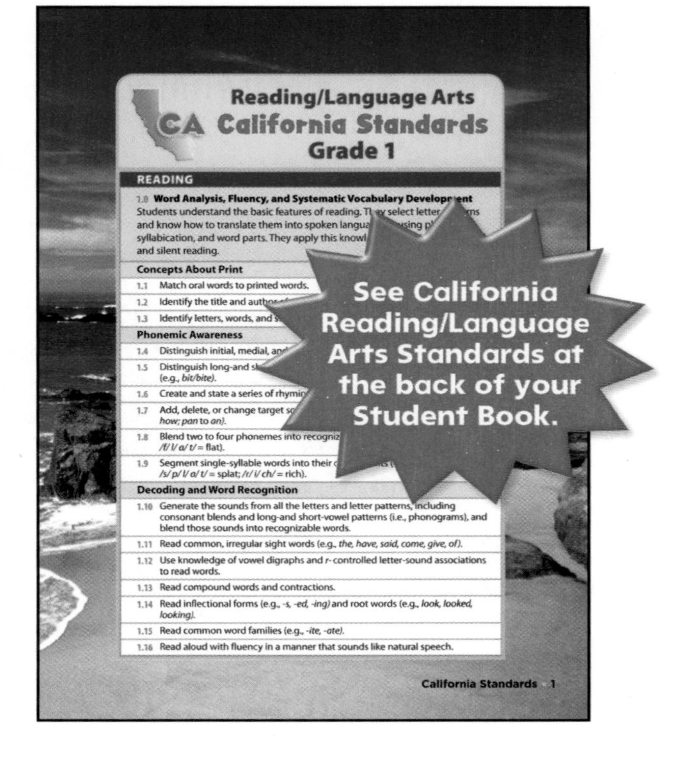

Reading/Language Arts
CA California Standards
Grade 1

READING

1.0 **Word Analysis, Fluency, and Systematic Vocabulary Development** Students understand the basic features of reading. They select letter patterns and know how to translate them into spoken language using ph... syllabication, and word parts. They apply this knowl... and silent reading.

Concepts About Print

1.1	Match oral words to printed words.
1.2	Identify the title and author...
1.3	Identify letters, words, and s...

Phonemic Awareness

1.4	Distinguish initial, medial, and...
1.5	Distinguish long-and sh... (e.g., *bit/bite*).
1.6	Create and state a series of rhymin...
1.7	Add, delete, or change target so... *how; pan* to *an*).
1.8	Blend two to four phonemes into recogniz... /f/ l/ a/ t/ = flat).
1.9	Segment single-syllable words into their c... /s/ p/ l/ a/ t/ = splat; /r/ i/ ch/ = rich).

Decoding and Word Recognition

1.10	Generate the sounds from all the letters and letter patterns, including consonant blends and long-and short-vowel patterns (i.e., phonograms), and blend those sounds into recognizable words.
1.11	Read common, irregular sight words (e.g., *the, have, said, come, give, of*).
1.12	Use knowledge of vowel digraphs and *r*-controlled letter-sound associations to read words.
1.13	Read compound words and contractions.
1.14	Read inflectional forms (e.g., *-s, -ed, -ing*) and root words (e.g., *look, looked, looking*).
1.15	Read common word families (e.g., *-ite, -ate*).
1.16	Read aloud with fluency in a manner that sounds like natural speech.

California Standards 1

Macmillan/McGraw-Hill

Unit 6

Spotlight on Grade One

Adventures

THE BIG QUESTION

THEME: Let's Go Out!

Award Winning Author and Illustrator

THEME: I Can Do It

Award Winning Author and Illustrator

THEME: At Work

THEME: Let's Find Out

THEME: Special Days

STANDARDS PRACTICE: Show What You Know

Unit 6
Adventures

What kinds of adventures can we have on any day?

Theme Launcher Video

Find out more about adventures at **www.macmillanmh.com**.

What kinds of adventures can we have on any day?

Have you ever had an adventure? We can have adventures every day. Sometimes adventures are fun, such as visiting a new place or seeing something special. Sometimes adventures can be hard, such as when you try something for the first time. How did you feel on your first day of school or the first time you tried to swim?

Sometimes adventures can be great! Whenever you learn something new it can be an adventure. We can also have adventures in our imaginations. What kinds of adventures have you had?

Research Activities

As you learn about adventures, think of an adventure you have had. How was it like the adventures you are reading about? Choose one of the stories you read. Then write about how your adventure was like the one in the story.

Keep Track of Ideas

As you read, write down your ideas about adventures on the Layered Book organizer. Write about the adventures you read about each week. Think about how these adventures are like adventures you have had.

FOLDABLES® Study Organizer

Adventures
Week 1
Week 2
Week 3
Week 4
Week 5

Research Toolkit

Conduct Your Unit 6 Research Online with:

Research Roadmap
Follow step-by-step guide to complete your research project.

Online Resources

- Topic Finder and other Research Tools
- Videos and Virtual Fieldtrips
- Photos and Drawings for Presentations
- Related Articles and Web Resources

California Web Site Links

Go to **www.macmillanmh.com** for more information.

California People

Tiger Woods, Golf Champion

Tiger Woods is the youngest golf champion ever. He started playing golf at the age of two and won many championships while still a teenager. In his spare time, Tiger works hard to help children.

Let's Go OUT!

CA Talk About It

What fun places have you visited? What did you do there?

LOG ON Find out more about special places at **www.macmillanmh.com**.

Words to Know

always
mother
father
love
four

---

firm
supposed

Read to Find Out

How is Joan's bedtime like your bedtime?

We Love Joan

Joan **always** stays up late.
She likes to sing songs that
she makes up. Her **mother**
and **father** try to get her
to sleep.

"We must be **firm** with her,"
they both say. "She is **supposed**
to go to bed."

"Joan," says Mother, "No more
songs. You must go to bed."

"We **love** you," say Mother
and Father.

"I love you too," sings Joan.

She sings it **four** more times.
Then she jumps into bed.

Comprehension

Genre

A Fantasy is a made-up story that could not really happen.

Visualize

Fantasy and Reality

Use your Fantasy and Reality Chart.

Reality	Fantasy
What Could Happen?	What Could Not Happen?

Read to Find Out

What kind of pig is Olivia?

written and illustrated by Ian Falconer

This is Olivia.
She is good at lots of things.

She is *very* good at wearing people out.

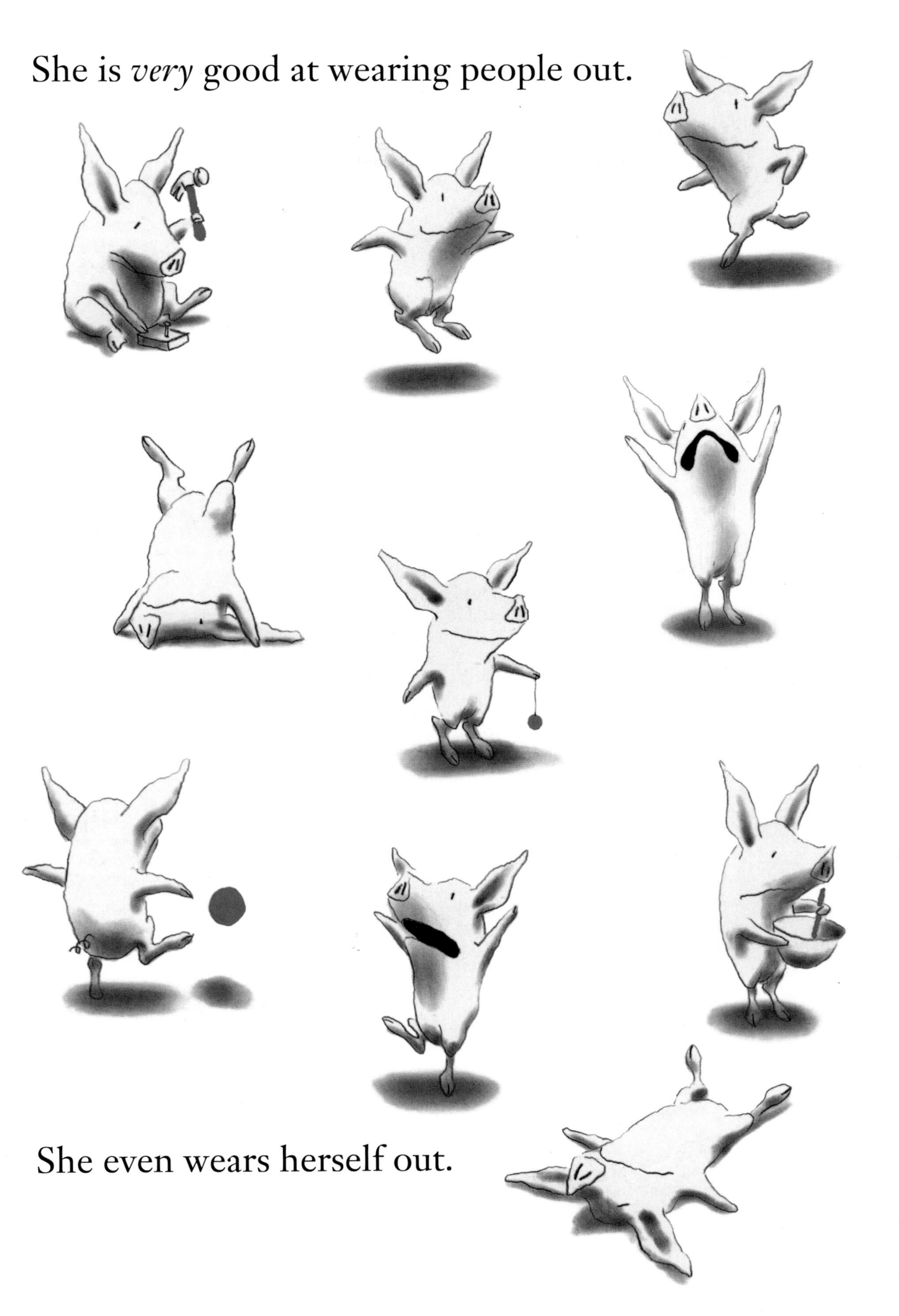

She even wears herself out.

Olivia has a little brother named Ian.
He's **always** copying.

Sometimes Ian just won't leave her alone,
so Olivia has to be **firm**.

Olivia lives with her **mother**, her **father**,
her brother, her dog, Perry,

and Edwin, the cat.

In the morning, after she gets up,
and moves the cat,

and brushes her teeth,
and combs her ears,

and moves the cat,

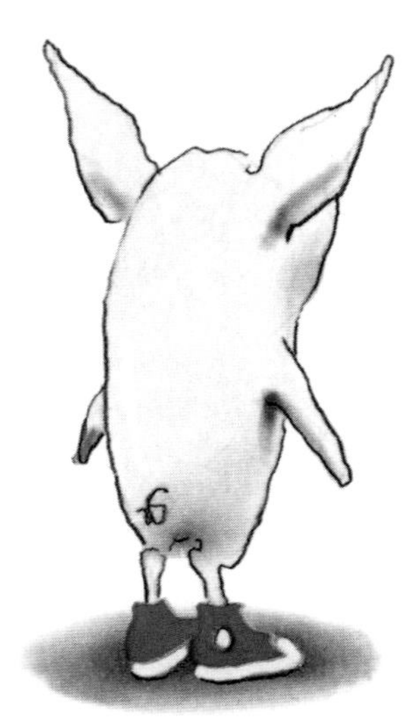

Olivia gets dressed.

She has to try on everything.

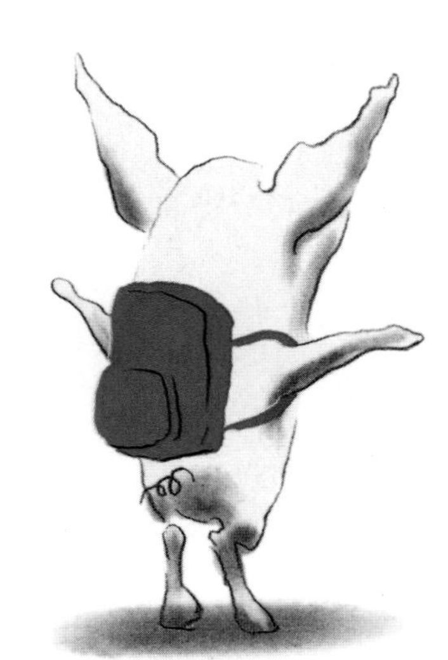

On sunny days, Olivia likes to go to the beach.

She feels it's important
to come prepared.

Last summer when Olivia was little, her
mother showed her how to make sand castles.

She got pretty good.

Sometimes Olivia
likes to bask in
the sun.

When her mother sees that she's had
enough, they go home.

Every day Olivia is **supposed** to take a nap.

"It's time for your you-know-what," her mother says.

Of course Olivia's not at all sleepy.

On rainy days, Olivia likes to go to the museum.

She heads straight for her favorite picture.

Olivia looks at it for a long time.

What could she be thinking?

But there is one painting Olivia just doesn't get.

"I could do that in about five minutes," she says to her mother.

As soon as she gets home, she gives it a try.

Time out.

After a nice bath, and a nice dinner, it's time for bed.

But of course Olivia's not at all sleepy.

"Only five books tonight, Mommy," she says.

"No, Olivia, just one."

"How about **four**?"

"Two."

"Three."

"Oh, all right, three.
But that's *it*!"

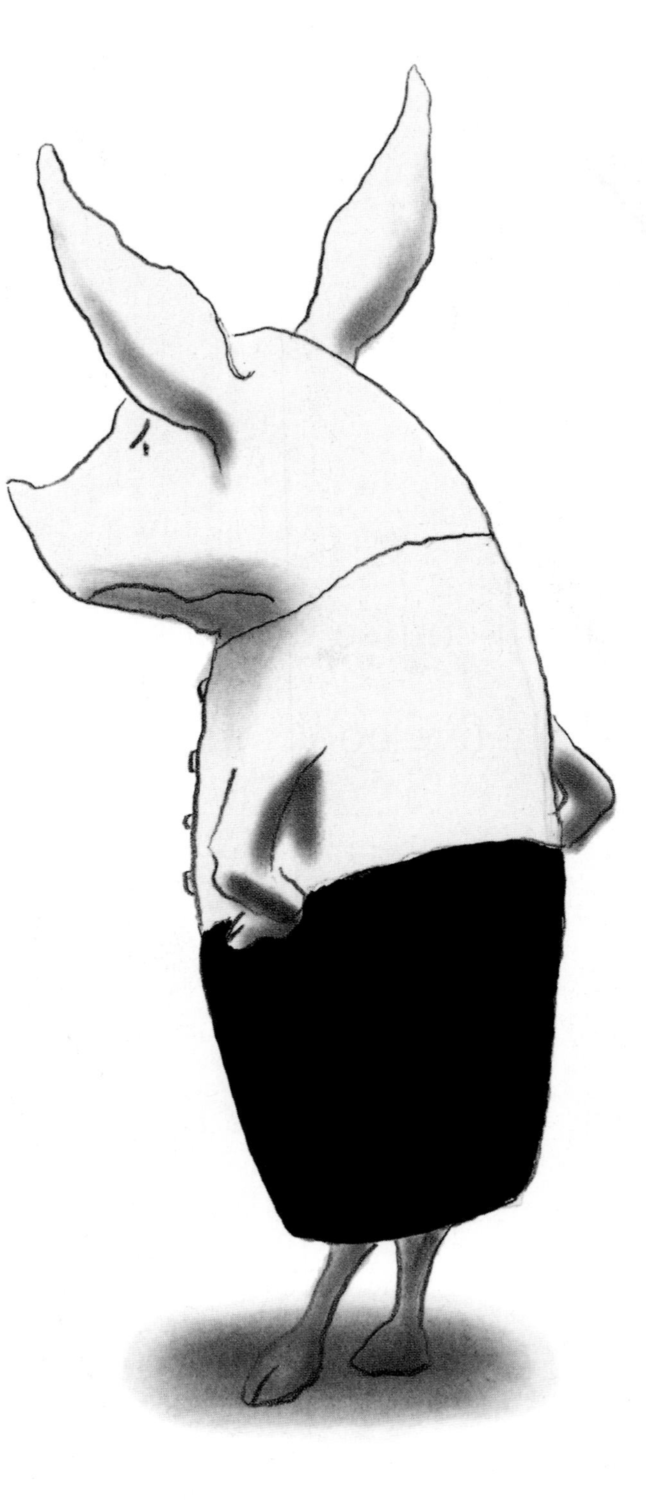

When they've finished reading, Olivia's mother gives her a kiss and says, "You know, you really wear me out. But I **love** you anyway."

And Olivia gives her a kiss back and says, "I love you anyway too."

READ TOGETHER

Meet Ian Falconer

Ian Falconer says the characters in his book are based on his sister's family. His niece, Olivia, is very busy and wears out her parents, just as Olivia in the story does. He decided to make Olivia a pig because he thinks pigs are very smart animals and that they're like humans in many ways.

Find out more about Ian Falconer at **www.macmillanmh.com**.

Other books by Ian Falconer

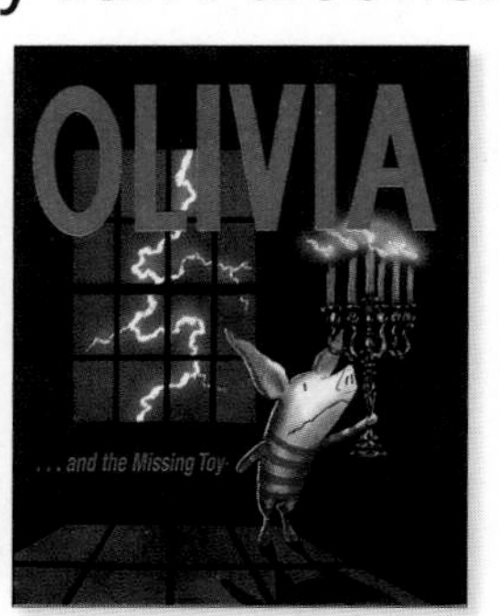

CA

Author Purpose

Ian Falconer wanted to write about a smart pig. Write about another smart animal. Tell why it's smart.

Critical Thinking

Retell the Story

Use the Retelling Cards to retell the story in order.

Retelling Cards

Think and Compare

Reality	Fantasy
What Could Happen?	What Could Not Happen?

1. Could this story happen in real life? Why or why not?
2. Do you ever act like Olivia? In what way?
3. Olivia likes to do creative things. What creative things do you like to do?
4. How are Olivia and Joan in "We Love Joan" alike?

CA History/Social Science

Genre
Nonfiction tells about real people and things.

Text Feature
A Caption gives information about a picture.

Content Vocabulary
artists
colors
sculpture

LOG ON Find out more about art at **www.macmillanmh.com**.

Cats in Art

Cats, cats, cats! Look at all the ways **artists** have shown cats.

This painting shows a cat at home. The artist used a lot of **colors** and shapes.

Orange Cat on Couch **was painted by Malcah Zeldis. She taught herself how to paint.**

What shape are the cat's ears?
What color is the cat?
Where else do you see that color?

This cat is not a painting. It is a **sculpture**. What shapes do you see? Why do you think this artist named this sculpture *The Rattle Cat*?

***The Rattle Cat* by Alexander Calder is made of metal.**

This sculpture of a cat and her kitten is very old. It comes from Egypt. How is this cat different from *The Rattle Cat*?

***Cat and Her Kitten* is more than 2,000 years old!**

Cat and Butterfly was painted with watercolors.

This cat was painted a long time ago. It comes from China. The cat is looking up. Can you see what it is looking at?

How would you show a cat? Make your own cat painting or sculpture!

CA **Critical Thinking**

Which cat in "Cats in Art" do you think would be Olivia's favorite? Why?

Write About a Place

CA **Writing**

Subjects and Predicates

The **subject** tells who or what a sentence is about. The **predicate** tells what the subject is or does.

Ryan wrote about seeing redwood trees.

Last summer, my family went to see the redwood trees. The trees were as big as buildings. Some trees were so wide you could drive a car through. The trees are very old. They may be more than 2,000 years old.

Your Turn

Write about an interesting place you have been.

Tell what you saw and did.

Tell what you learned.

Writer's Checklist

Did I write about an interesting place?

Did I tell what I saw and did? Did I include something I learned?

Does each sentence have a **subject** and a **predicate**?

CA

Talk About It

What is something hard that you have learned to do? How did you learn?

LOG ON Find out more about doing new things at **www.macmillanmh.com**.

I Can Do It

Words to Know

early

instead

thought

nothing

along

---

errand

suddenly

Read to Find Out

How does Cory feel at the end of the story?

Nothing Stops Cory

Cory woke up very **early**. **Instead** of going back to sleep, she got out of bed. "Today is the day I'm going to swim," she **thought**. "**Nothing** can stop me."

Mom had to do an **errand**. Then she drove Cory to her swim class. **Suddenly** Cory was in the water **along** with her teacher, Shelly.

Shelly held Cory's hands as she kicked. Then she let go. Cory was swimming! "This is the best sport for me," she thought.

Comprehension

Genre

Realistic Fiction is a made-up story that could really happen.

Ask Questions

Make Inferences

Use your Inference Chart.

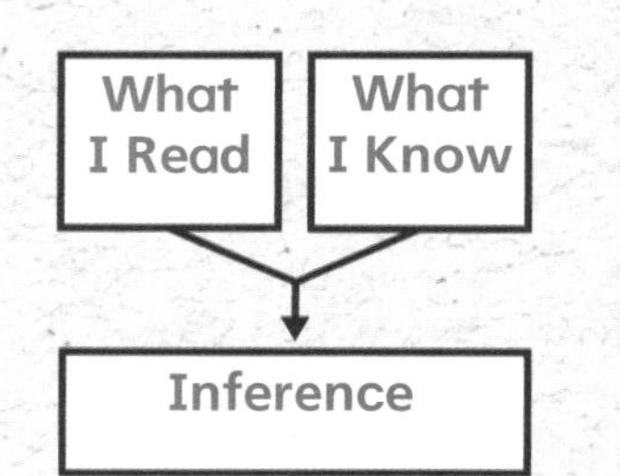

Read to Find Out

How does Peter feel about learning to whistle?

Whistle for Willie

Award Winning Author and Illustrator

by Ezra Jack Keats

Oh, how Peter wished he could whistle!

He saw a boy playing with his dog. Whenever the boy whistled, the dog ran straight to him.

Peter tried to whistle, but he couldn't.
So **instead** he began to turn himself around—
around and around he whirled ...
faster and faster....

When he stopped
everything turned
down …
and up …

and up …
and down …
and around
and around.

Peter saw his dog, Willie, coming.
Quick as a wink, he hid in an empty
carton lying on the sidewalk.

"Wouldn't it be funny if I whistled?" Peter **thought**.
"Willie would stop and look all around to see
who it was."

Peter tried again to whistle—but still he couldn't.
So Willie just walked on.

Peter got out of the carton
and started home.
On the way he took some
colored chalks out of his pocket
and drew a long, long line
right up to his door.

He stood there and tried to whistle again.
He blew till his cheeks were tired.
But **nothing** happened.

He went into his house and put on his father's old hat to make himself feel more grown up. He looked into the mirror to practice whistling.
Still no whistle!

When his mother saw what he was doing, Peter pretended that he was his father.

He said, "I've come home **early** today, dear. Is Peter here?"

His mother answered, “Why no, he’s outside with Willie.”

“Well, I’ll go out and look for them,” said Peter.

ME
CAT

First he walked **along** a crack in the sidewalk. Then he tried to run away from his shadow.

He jumped off his shadow,
but when he landed they were
together again.

He came to the corner where the carton was, and who should he see but Willie!

Peter scrambled under the carton.
He blew and blew and blew.
Suddenly—out came a real whistle!

Willie stopped and looked around to see who it was.

“It’s me,” Peter shouted, and stood up.
Willie raced straight to him.

Peter ran home to show his father and mother what he could do. They loved Peter's whistling. So did Willie.

Peter's mother asked him and Willie to go on an **errand** to the grocery store.

Willie stopped and looked around to see who it was.

“It’s me,” Peter shouted, and stood up.
Willie raced straight to him.

He whistled all the way there,
and he whistled all the way home.

READ TOGETHER

Getting to Know Ezra Jack Keats

Ezra Jack Keats sold his first painting when he was eight years old! When he grew up, he created many books for children. He used cut-out paper and a special type of paste to make the bright pictures. He won many awards for his work, but he was most pleased by letters from children who had read his books.

Other books by Ezra Jack Keats

LOG ON Find out more about Ezra Jack Keats at **www.macmillanmh.com**.

CA Author's Purpose

Ezra Jack Keats wanted to write about a boy who wished he could whistle. Write about something you wish you could do. Tell why you want to do it.

Critical Thinking

Retelling Cards

Retell the Story

Use the Retelling Cards to retell the story in order.

Think and Compare

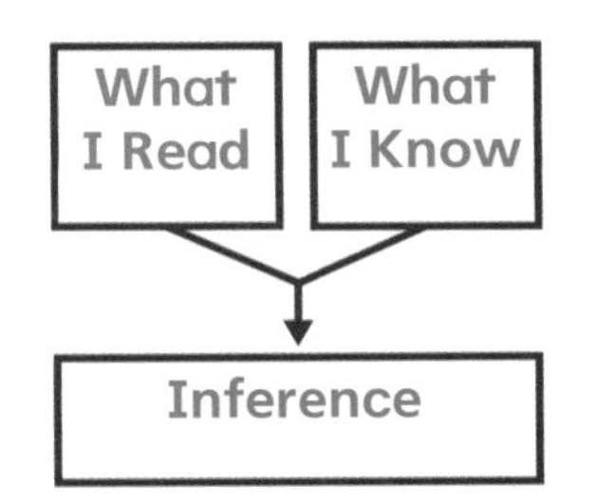

1. How do you think Peter feels about Willie?
2. Would you like to have Peter as your friend? Tell why or why not.
3. How is Willie a good pet?
4. What do Cory in "Nothing Stops Cory" and Peter both learn?

Seeing-Eye DOGS

History/
Social Science

Genre
Nonfiction gives information about a topic.

Text Feature
A List is a series of items written down in a certain order.

Content Vocabulary
guide
harness
commands

LOG ON Find out more about seeing-eye dogs at **www.macmillanmh.com**.

Most dogs are pets, but some dogs have jobs. Seeing-eye dogs have a very special job. They help people who can't see.

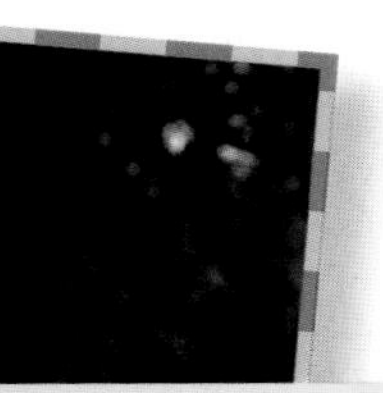

Traits of a Guide Dog

1. It is smart.
2. It likes people.
3. It is the right size.
4. It is kind.
5. It is in good shape.

Seeing-eye dogs are also called **guide** dogs. These dogs guide, or lead, blind people. The dogs can help them get anyplace they want.

How do guide dogs learn this job? Their training starts when they are six weeks old. They go to live with a puppy raiser who takes care of them for a year.

If a puppy shows it can learn fast, it will go to a special school. That is when the real training starts!

At school, the dogs learn a lot. They get used to wearing a **harness**. They learn how to lead someone on a sidewalk. They learn how to cross a street and ride a bus. When they finish school, they can follow 20 **commands**!

Next, the dog meets its new owner. They must learn how to work with each other. They are trained together at the school for four weeks. Then it is time to go home. They are now a team!

CA **Critical Thinking**

What kind of guide dog do you think Willie would make?

CA **Writing**

Pronouns

A **pronoun** is a word that replaces a noun.

Write a How-To

Ravi wrote about how to play a game.

How to Play Mix Six

1. Write a sentence. It should have six words.
2. Cut the words apart and mix them up.
3. Tell your friend to put the sentence back together.

hid under box the Peter big

Your Turn

Think of something new
you have learned this year.

Think of how you learned it.

Write to explain what you
learned.

Writer's Checklist

 Are my directions clear?

 Are my sentences in the right order?

 Did I use each **pronoun** correctly?

Talk About It

What jobs do you know about? What jobs would you like to do?

LOG ON Find out more about jobs at **www.macmillanmh.com**.

At Work

TIME
FOR KIDS®

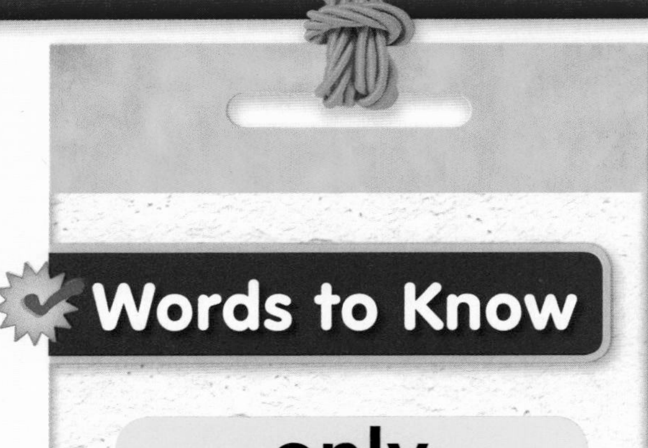

only

laugh

build

goes

---

interesting

ordinary

Do you ever think about what you want to be? You could find an **interesting** job. You **only** need to think about what you like!

Do you like to help people? You could be a doctor or a teacher. Do you like to make people **laugh**? You could be a clown or an actor. Do you like to fix things? You could **build** houses or fix cars.

You could work at home. Or you could be someone who **goes** to the moon. You could want a job that seems **ordinary**, or one that does not. Think about what you like to do. Then you can find your best job!

CA Comprehension

Genre
Nonfiction
A nonfiction article tells about real people and things.

Reread
Classify and Categorize
What different kinds of jobs do people have?

Cool Jobs

What would it be like to have these three jobs?

Zoo Dentist

If you were a zoo dentist, you could fix and clean a tiger's teeth. You could fill a hole in an alligator's tooth. You might even pull out an elephant's tusk!

Zoo dentists fix teeth just as **ordinary** dentists do. But they work on wild animals that might bite! So the dentist gives medicine to the animal. Then it **goes** to sleep. Now the dentist can go to work.

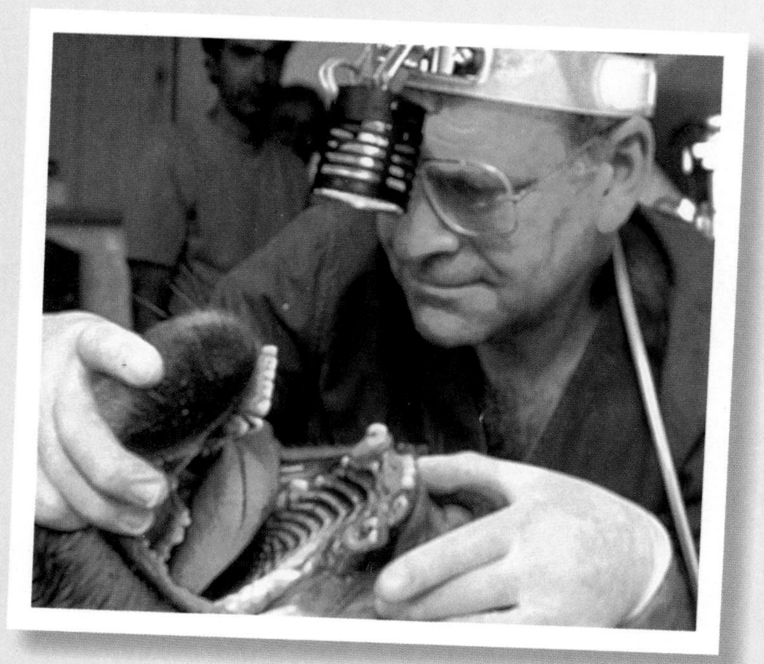

Zoo dentists use big drills to clean out holes in teeth. Big metal tools can help them grip a bad tooth and pull it out. If it's a lion tooth, that can be a pretty big job!

Flavor Maker

Did you ever want to change the taste of a food? If you were a flavor maker, you could! You could make medicine taste like cherry or pizza. With **only** a few drops, you could make a hot dog taste like a peach.

Flavor makers work in a lab. They use chemicals to make flavors. Their best tools are their noses and mouths. They do a lot of tasting and smelling!

Flavor makers help make a lot of tasty food! Can you think of a new flavor for a food that you like?

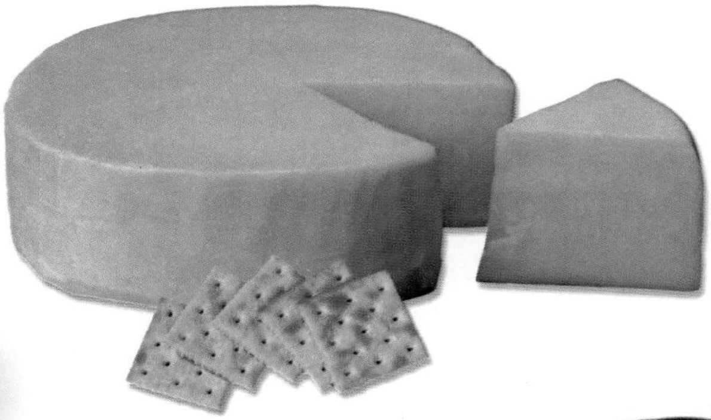

Cheese-flavored crackers

Cherry-flavored medicine

Fruit-flavored cereal

Beekeeper

Bees make honey. A beekeeper helps the bees do their job.

If you were a beekeeper, you would **build** hives for bees to live in. These are not like the hives bees make themselves. Beekeepers make hives out of wood.

How do beekeepers get the honey with all of those stinging bees? They have special outfits to keep the bees from stinging them. There are gloves and a hood. There is a net that protects the beekeeper's face.

Sometimes beekeepers put smoke into the hives. That makes the bees fly away. Then the beekeepers can take the honey out. It can take a lot of work to get honey. But the end is always sweet!

There are many **interesting** jobs in the world. This person's job is to dress up like a huge bird and perform at sports events. It's fun to make people **laugh**.

What kinds of cool jobs can you think of? What cool job would you like to have?

CA Critical Thinking

Tell What You Learned

What different kinds of jobs did you learn about?

Think and Compare

1. Which jobs in "Cool Jobs" are about making things? Which jobs are about helping?
2. Which job in "Cool Jobs" was most interesting to you? Why?
3. What makes a job a good job?
4. How are the jobs in "A Job for You" like the jobs in "Cool Jobs"? How are they different?

Jobs at School

CA **Show What You Know**

Author and Me
Think about what the author tells you. Think about what you know.

Would you like a job at a school? Teaching is a fun job. But there are a lot of other good jobs at school, too.

You might like to be a school nurse. A nurse takes care of sick kids. A nurse can bandage cuts and scrapes.

Do you like to fix things? You might like to be a custodian. A custodian keeps things clean. A custodian fixes things that are broken.

Do you like cooking? Then you might like a job in the lunchroom. A cook makes sure the kids have good food to eat.

There are a lot of fun jobs at school. But the best part is being with so many kids!

Go on 

Directions: Answer the questions.

1 What is this story MAINLY about?

A kids going to school

B eating good foods

C working in a school

Tip
Think about what you know.

2 Who can help you if your chair breaks?

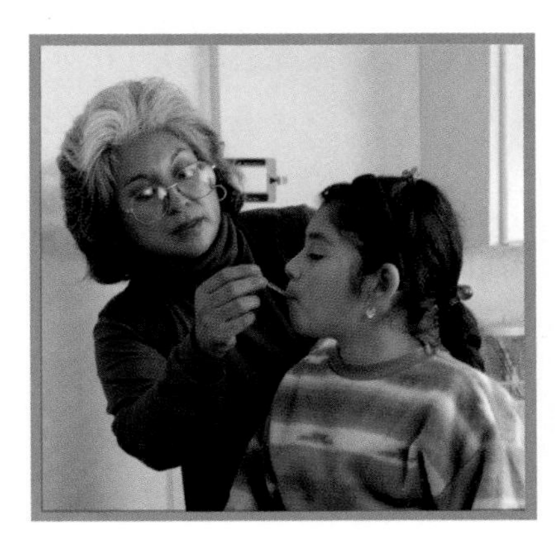

A

B

C

3 You know from reading this story that

A many people work in schools.

B only teachers work in schools.

C nurses help cook good foods.

Write About an Interesting Job

Edgar wrote about a job that he thinks is interesting. He made sure his sentences were clear.

Driving a bulldozer is a very good job. Bulldozers help make roads and buildings. They are very strong. Driving a bulldozer is fun. You push dirt and rocks around. You even get to push down buildings.

CA Your Writing Prompt

There are lots of different jobs.

Think about a job that is interesting to you.

Write a report telling why you are interested in that job.

Writing Hints

Write about what you think the job would be like. Tell why you would like it.

Read your sentences over to make sure they make sense.

Check your report for mistakes.

Let's Find Out

Talk About It

What topic do you want to know about? How would you find out about it?

Find out more about learning new things at **www.macmillanmh.com**.

Words to Know

gone

been

before

searching

---

clues

invisible

Read to Find Out

How does Freddy's friend help him?

Where Has Freddy Gone Now?

Fern and Freddy were best friends. So Fern was upset when she couldn't find him.

"Where has he **gone**?" she said. "He has never **been** lost **before**. I must start **searching** for him!"

Fern went from one end of the pond to the other. But she couldn't find any **clues**.

"He's not **invisible**," she said.

Then there was a sudden shout. It was Freddy! He was trapped in a web. In a flash, Fern pulled him out.

"Let's get out of here!" said Freddy, and off they went.

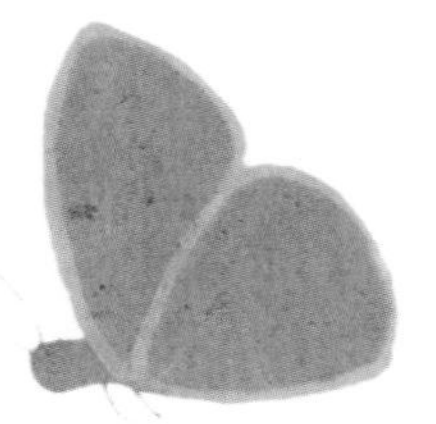

Comprehension

Genre
In a **Mystery**, the characters use clues to figure something out.

Reread
Make Predictions
Use your Predictions Chart.

What I Predict	What Happens

Read to Find Out
Where do Dot and Jabber find bugs?

Dot and Jabber and the Big Bug Mystery

by Ellen Stoll Walsh

Dot and Jabber, the mouse detectives, were looking for a mystery to solve. They walked through the meadow and stopped to watch some bugs.

The mice thought they heard something. They turned to see, and when they turned back, the bugs had disappeared.

"Wow," said Jabber. "The bugs vanished. Poof!"

"They must be around here someplace," said Dot. "They couldn't have **gone** away so fast."

"Then they're **invisible**," said Jabber. "I can't see them at all, and I'm looking."

"Come on, Jabber," said Dot. "This is the mystery we've **been** looking for. Let's find those bugs! We need to look for **clues**."

"Dot, listen," Jabber whispered. "I think I hear one."

"One what?" said Dot.

"One clue. *Shhh.* Let's go check."

The mice crept over the hill.

"It's a sparrow," Jabber said. "No wonder the bugs disappeared. Sparrows eat bugs."

"Not me," the sparrow said. "I'm going to find some berries. They don't vanish when you want one."

And he hopped off.

"Now that the sparrow is gone," said Dot,
"why don't the bugs come back?"

"They're hiding from the toad," said a rabbit.
"Toads eat bugs, too."

“Where is the toad?” said Dot.

“Hiding from things that eat toads,” said the rabbit.

“I don’t get it,” said Jabber. “Everybody’s hiding, but I don’t see anyplace to hide.”

"Maybe we don't know how to look," said Dot. "Let's keep **searching**. The bugs can't be far away."

"They're watching us," said Jabber. "I can feel it."

"I can, too," said Dot.

"This gives me goose bumps," said Jabber. "They can see us, but we can't see them. I wonder what else is out there watching us?"

Dot caught her breath. "Jabber, quick. Something moved."

"I don't see it," said Jabber.

"Look," said Dot. "It's moving again."

Some butterflies rose from the meadow and flew away.

"Wow, butterflies!" said Jabber. "I think the butterflies are a clue. They were hiding in plain sight, and we didn't even see them. Maybe the other bugs are hiding in plain sight, too."

"Oh!" said Dot. "Do you mean they're pretending to look like something else? Let's see if you're right."

"Dot," said Jabber. "Do rocks breathe?"

"Of course not," said Dot.

"Then I've found the toad."

"Jabber," said Dot. "I found the bugs!"

"*Shhh*," said a grasshopper.

"You're right, Dot. There are lots of bugs here!" said Jabber. "We just have to know how to look."

The grasshopper sighed. “Go ahead. Tell the toad where we are. Tell the whole world. What are a few bugs, more or less? I’m out of here.”

“Wait for us!” said the other bugs.

"Well," said Dot, "the bugs have really disappeared now. But not **before** the great mouse detectives solved another mystery!" Dot looked around. "Jabber, where are you?"

"Try to find me," said Jabber. "I'm hiding in plain sight!"

READ TOGETHER

Making Pictures with Ellen Stoll Walsh

Ellen Stoll Walsh says, "We have always loved stories in my family." When she started reading stories to her son, she decided to write and make pictures for children's stories, too. She often makes the animals in her books out of cut paper. She uses colored ink for her drawings.

Other books by Ellen Stoll Walsh

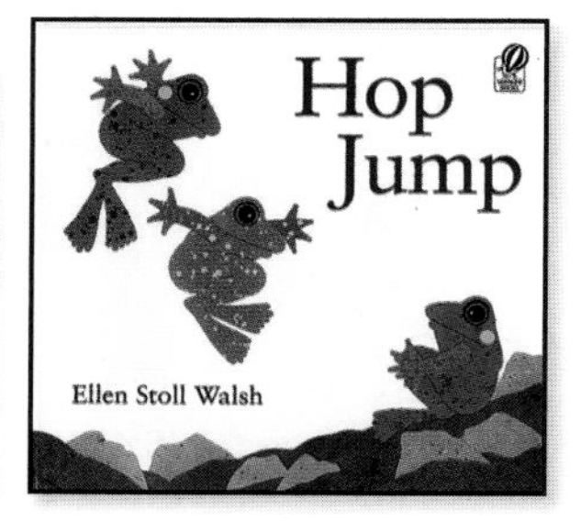

Author's Purpose

Ellen Stoll Walsh wanted to write about mice. Write about an animal you like. Tell about where it lives.

Critical Thinking

Retell the Story

Use the Retelling Cards to retell the story in order.

Retelling Cards

Think and Compare

What I Predict	What Happens

1. Where did you predict Dot and Jabber would find the bugs?
2. What part of the story did you like best? Tell why.
3. Why do the bugs in the story seem to disappear? Have you seen other animals disappear like that?
4. How might Dot and Jabber look for Freddy in "Where Has Freddy Gone Now?"

CA **Science**

Genre
Nonfiction gives information about a topic.

Text Feature
A Head tells what information is in a section.

Content Vocabulary
insects
protects
senses

LOG ON Find out more about insects at **www.macmillanmh.com**.

The World of Insects

Insects are everywhere. There are more **insects** than any other kind of animal.

Kinds of Insects

There are all kinds of insects. The ladybug, housefly, and ant are all insects.

Some insects can fly. Many insects can not. Some live in water. But most live on the land. Some kinds of insects live and work together, such as bees or ants. But most insects do not.

The Body of an Insect

All insects have six legs. All insects have three body parts. Insect bodies have no bones. The outside of an insect's body is hard. The hard outside **protects** its insides. Many insects have antennas.

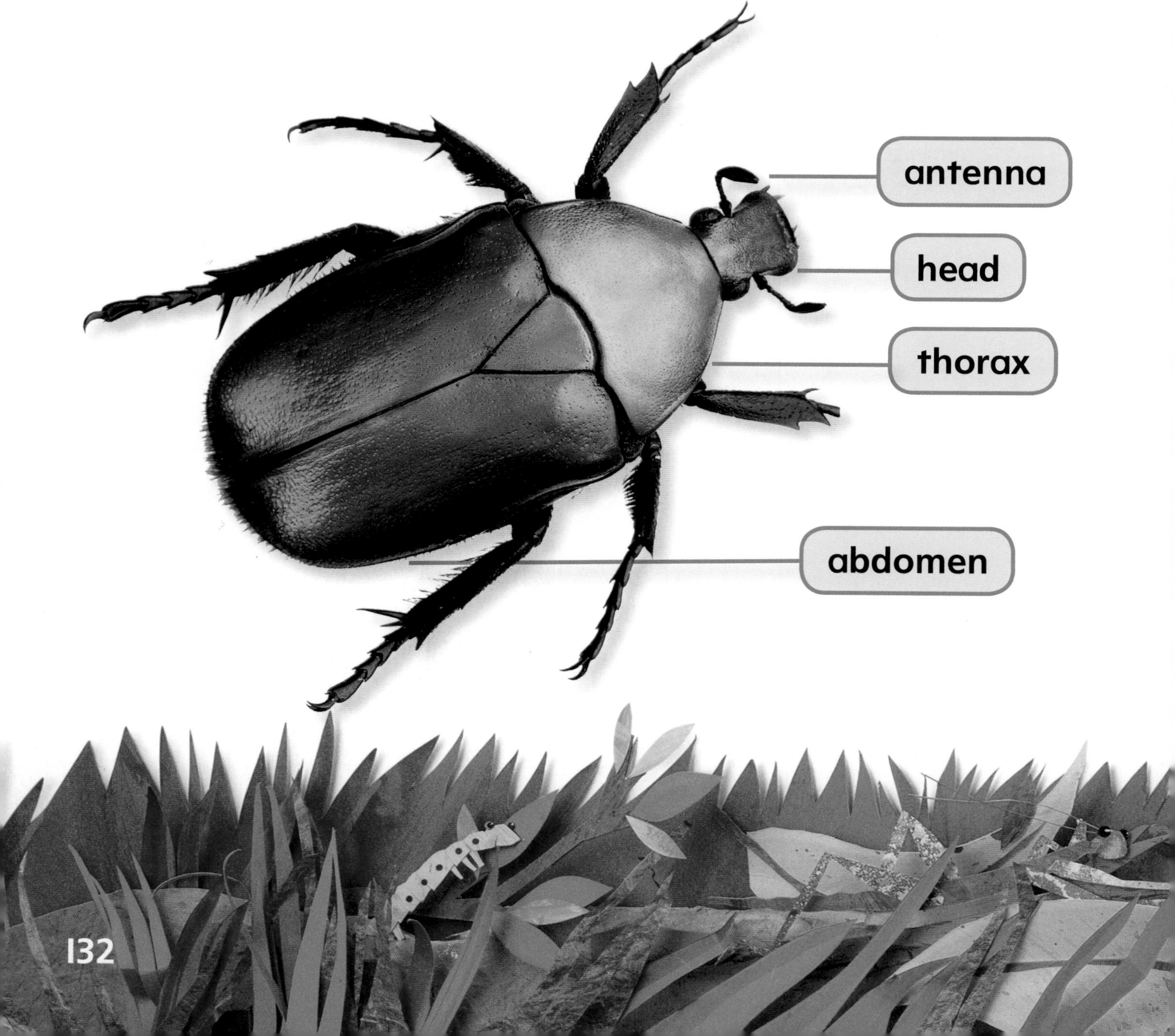

Insect Senses

Insect **senses** are not like people's senses. Many insects smell with their antennas. Bees taste with their antennas. Flies taste with their feet.

Insects do not see the same as we do. Some insects have more than two eyes. A grasshopper has five eyes. It can see on all sides.

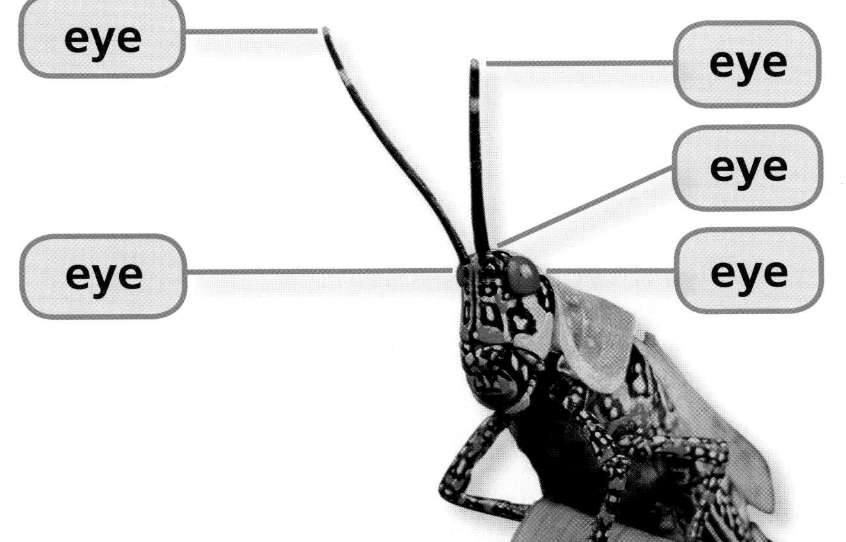

Critical Thinking

How are the insects in *Dot and Jabber and the Big Bug Mystery* like the insects in this piece?

Writing

Pronouns *I* and *Me*

Use **I** in the subject of a sentence. Use **me** in the predicate.

Write How to Make Something

Sasha wrote about making a butterfly.

I can make a butterfly!

My sister showed me how.

1. Fold a piece of paper.
2. Cut two half circles.
3. Unfold the paper.
4. Decorate your butterfly.

Your Turn

What do you know how to make?

Write how to make it. Be sure to include each step.

Tell how you learned to make it.

Writer's Checklist

 Will readers be able to follow my directions?

 Did I include each step?

 Did I use I and me correctly?

Special Days

Talk About It

What is a special day that you have had? What made it special?

LOG ON Find out more about special days at **www.macmillanmh.com**.

Words to Know

- around
- brought
- straight
- certain
- minutes
- begin

- daydream
- cancel

Read to Find Out

What will the party be like?

The Surprise Party

Ron is my best friend. He lives **around** the corner from me. We are on the same baseball team. We like to **daydream** about being baseball stars.

Today I am having a surprise party for Ron. Ron's mom **brought** the treats to my house. We are hanging "We Like Ron!" posters. It is my job to make sure the posters are **straight**.

All of Ron's friends are coming to the party. **Certain** grown-ups are coming too. Only one friend had to **cancel** because she was sick. Ron will be here in five **minutes**. Then the party will **begin**!

Comprehension

Genre

Fiction is a story that has been made up.

Story Structure

Character, Setting, Plot

Use your Story Chart.

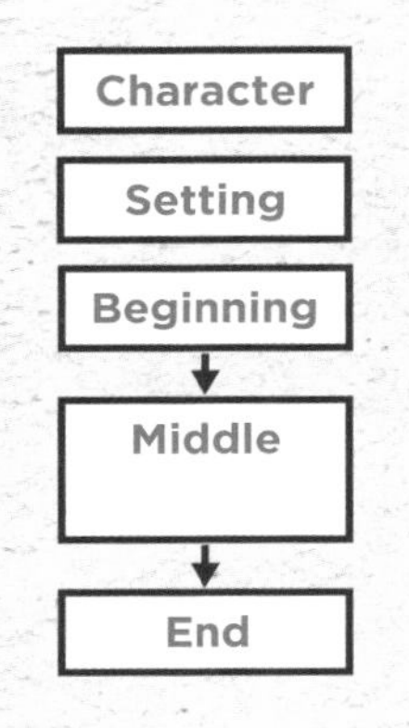

Read to Find Out

What happens when Oscar forgets to tell the neighbors about the picnic?

Super Oscar

By Oscar De La Hoya
with Mark Shulman
illustrated by Lisa Kopelke

Oscar was a daydreamer.

When Oscar rode the bus to school in the morning, he daydreamed the whole ride away. At school, Oscar would **daydream** **straight** through his lunchtime. And when he rode the bus home from school, he daydreamed some more.

At breakfast, Oscar daydreamed as his pancakes got cold and his orange juice got warm.

His father said, "Oscar, it's good to dream. But sometimes you need to take your head out of the clouds to get things done."

"Right," Oscar said.

On Saturdays in Oscar's neighborhood, everyone got together for a picnic in the park. People **brought** all sorts of food and there were games to play.

Oscar's mother was in charge of making the lists so that everyone knew what to bring. Oscar would run **around** his neighborhood to give out the lists. One week a **certain** daydreamer forgot to give them out.

That Saturday, Oscar was lying on the grass, looking at the shapes in the clouds.

His mother called, "OSCAR! You never gave out the lists! We'll have to **cancel** the picnic. There won't be anything to eat!"

"Don't worry, Mami!" Oscar said as he jumped up. "There's still time!"

And in a flash, Oscar zipped away. He rushed to the grocery store. He bought everything he needed and raced to the park.

Twenty minutes until the picnic....

Oscar quickly unpacked the groceries and set the picnic tables.

Fifteen minutes until the picnic....

Next, Oscar made up a humongous batch of guacamole following Tía Raquel's recipe … for the most part.

Ten minutes until the picnic....

Then Oscar began whipping up the cream for the strawberry shortcake dessert.

Five minutes until the picnic....

The clock struck noon. It was time for the picnic to **begin**. All of Oscar's friends and neighbors came into the park. Oscar was excited—until he realized there was no music!

Oscar taught a few friends a tune. They performed it beautifully as everyone was arriving at the picnic site.

This picnic started with Oscar's favorite event—the empanada-eating contest.

It was the best picnic ever.

By the time the strawberry shortcake was served that afternoon, Oscar was nowhere to be found.

Sweet dreams, Oscar.

Read Together

Meet the Real Super Oscar

The real Oscar De La Hoya is a super athlete. He is famous all over the world for his skill in boxing. As a child, Oscar went to school in East Los Angeles. His real dream is to make good schools for kids from that neighborhood. Like Oscar in the story, he has a lot of energy and likes to help out!

LOG ON Find out more about Oscar De La Hoya at **www.macmillanmh.com**.

CA Author's Purpose

The real Super Oscar likes to take on big challenges. Write about another challenge little Super Oscar could take on.

CA Critical Thinking

Retell the Story

Use the Retelling Cards to retell the story in order.

Retelling Cards

Think and Compare

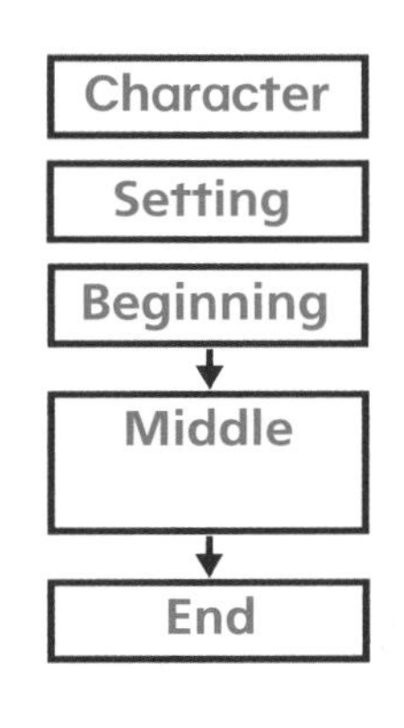

1. How does Oscar get the picnic ready in time? What special skills does he use?

2. Did you ever forget to do something as Oscar did? What happened?

3. What parts of this story could not happen in real life?

4. How is Oscar's day like the children's day in "The Surprise Party"?

Read Together

CA

Poetry

Genre
Poetry uses rhythm and rhyme to make words fun to say.

Literary Element
Many poems have a Rhyming Pattern. In some poems, the second line in a verse rhymes with the fourth line.

LOG ON Find out more at www.macmillanmh.com.

Dancing Paper

by Pat Mora

Let's fill the room with laughing
before our friends arrive.
We'll bring the colored paper.
The room will come alive.

Let's start with the *piñata*.
The air will sway and swing.
We'll string *papel picado*
to start its fluttering.

I'll fling the *serpentinas*,
toss coils in the air.
We'll add *marimba* music,
start dancing everywhere.

Remember *cascarones*,
to hide will be in vain.
Egg-bursts of bright confetti
will shower us like rain.

CA Critical Thinking

How is the special day in *Super Oscar* like the day described in "Dancing Paper"?

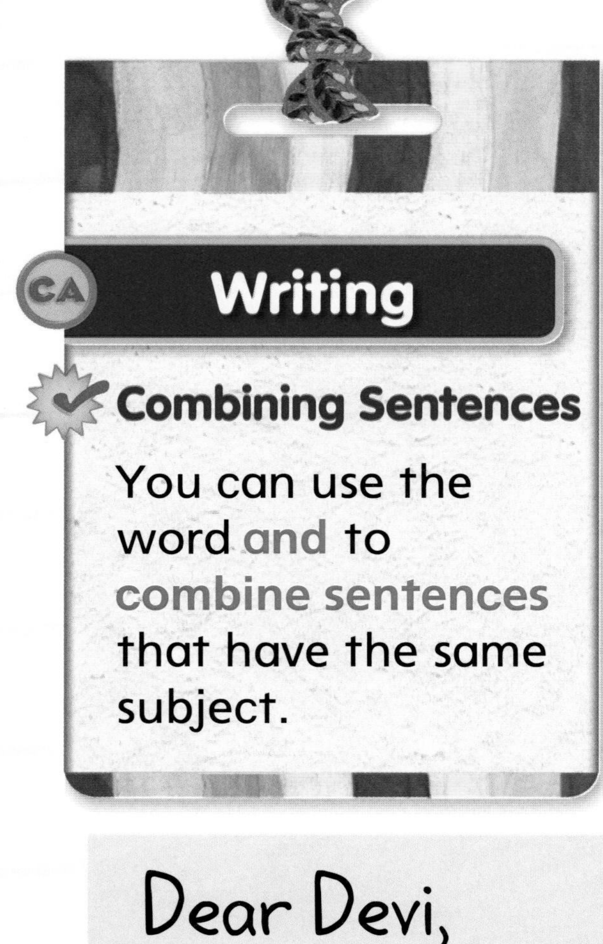

Write a Letter

Isabel wrote a letter about a special day.

Dear Devi,

Today my cousin Marcus came home to visit. We all went to his house. I helped cook lunch and hang up decorations. Then the cousins all sang and danced. It was so much fun!

Yours truly,

Isabel

Welcome Home!

Your Turn

Think about a special day you have had.

Write a letter to a friend to tell about the day.

Include details that tell what you did and how you felt.

Writer's Checklist

Did I include details about my special day?

Did I use **and** to **combine sentences** that have the same subject?

Does my letter begin with a greeting and end with a closing?

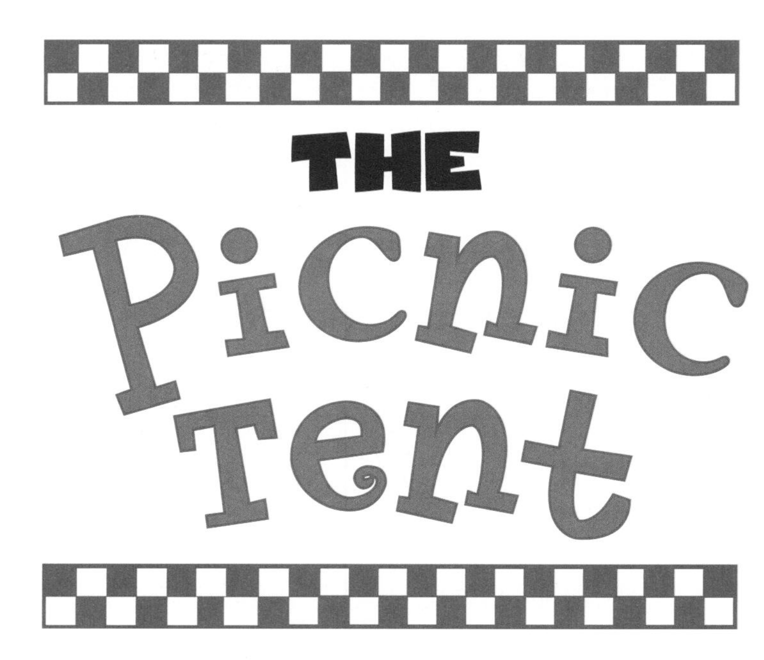

THE Picnic Tent

Jen and James packed a picnic for the park. They put peanut butter and jelly sandwiches and drinks in a basket. Jen put their lunch and a plastic tablecloth on her bike. James put their kites, a ball, and two books of mazes in his backpack.

At the park, Jen and James flew their kites. They played catch. But then it began to rain.

"It's too soon to go home," said James.

"I have an idea!" said Jen. She removed the plastic cloth from the table. She put it under the table. Then she and James ate lunch and did mazes until it stopped raining.

Life of a Butterfly

Where do butterflies come from? A butterfly begins life as an egg. When the egg hatches, a caterpillar crawls out. It crawls on leaves and it uses them for food. As it eats, it grows. As it gets bigger, it changes in other ways.

The caterpillar hangs upside down from a leaf or a stalk. Next, it makes a hard shell around itself. Inside, the caterpillar changes more. Now it is called a pupa.

In about ten days, the pupa's shell cracks. A butterfly comes out. At first, its wings are wet. When its wings dry, the butterfly flies away. It begins a new life.

Most butterflies live from one to two weeks. Some may live for a year.

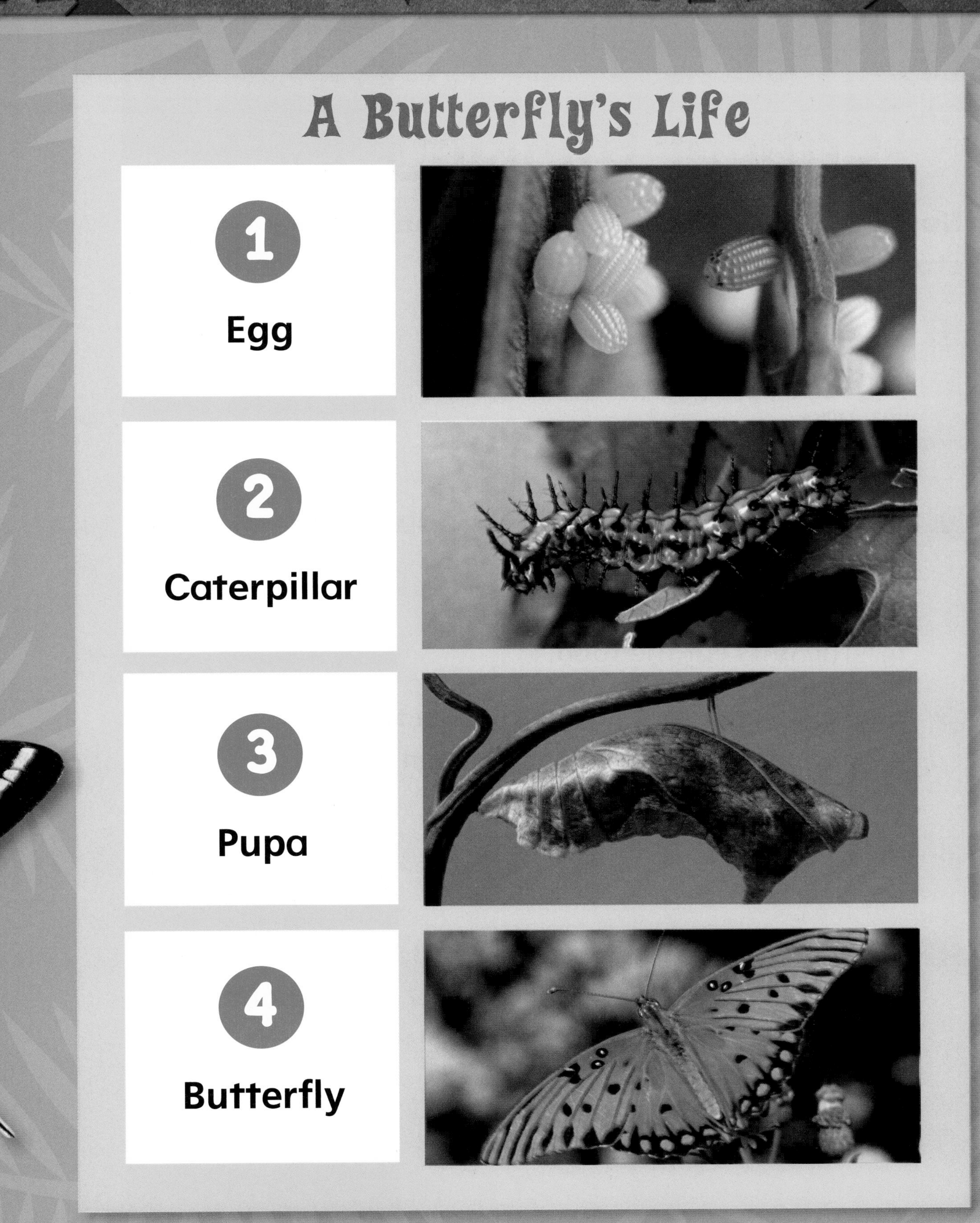
A Butterfly's Life
1
Egg
2
Caterpillar
3
Pupa
4
Butterfly

Critical Thinking

Now answer the questions. Base your answers on the story "The Picnic Tent."

1 What is the SETTING of this story?

A school

B park

C home

2 What problem happens in the MIDDLE of the story?

A James scrapes his arm.

B It starts to rain.

C The ants eat the food.

3 Jen removed the plastic cloth from the table. What does the word removed mean?

A fell asleep

B took off

C cleaned off

4 What did you PREDICT James and Jen would do when it began to rain? What did they do? Write about it.

Now answer the questions. Base your answers on the story "Life of a Butterfly."

1 What comes out of a butterfly egg?

A a butterfly

B a caterpillar

C another egg

2 What does the caterpillar turn into next?

A a pupa

B a butterfly

C a bird

3 What does the caption tell about butterflies?

A how big they grow to

B how long they live

C what colors they are

Write on Demand

PROMPT Tell how a butterfly grows. Use your own words. Write as much as you can and as well as you can.

Glossary

What Is a Glossary?

A glossary can help you find the meanings of words. The words are listed in alphabetical order. You can look up a word and read it in a sentence. Sometimes there is a picture.

insects

colors

Sample Entry

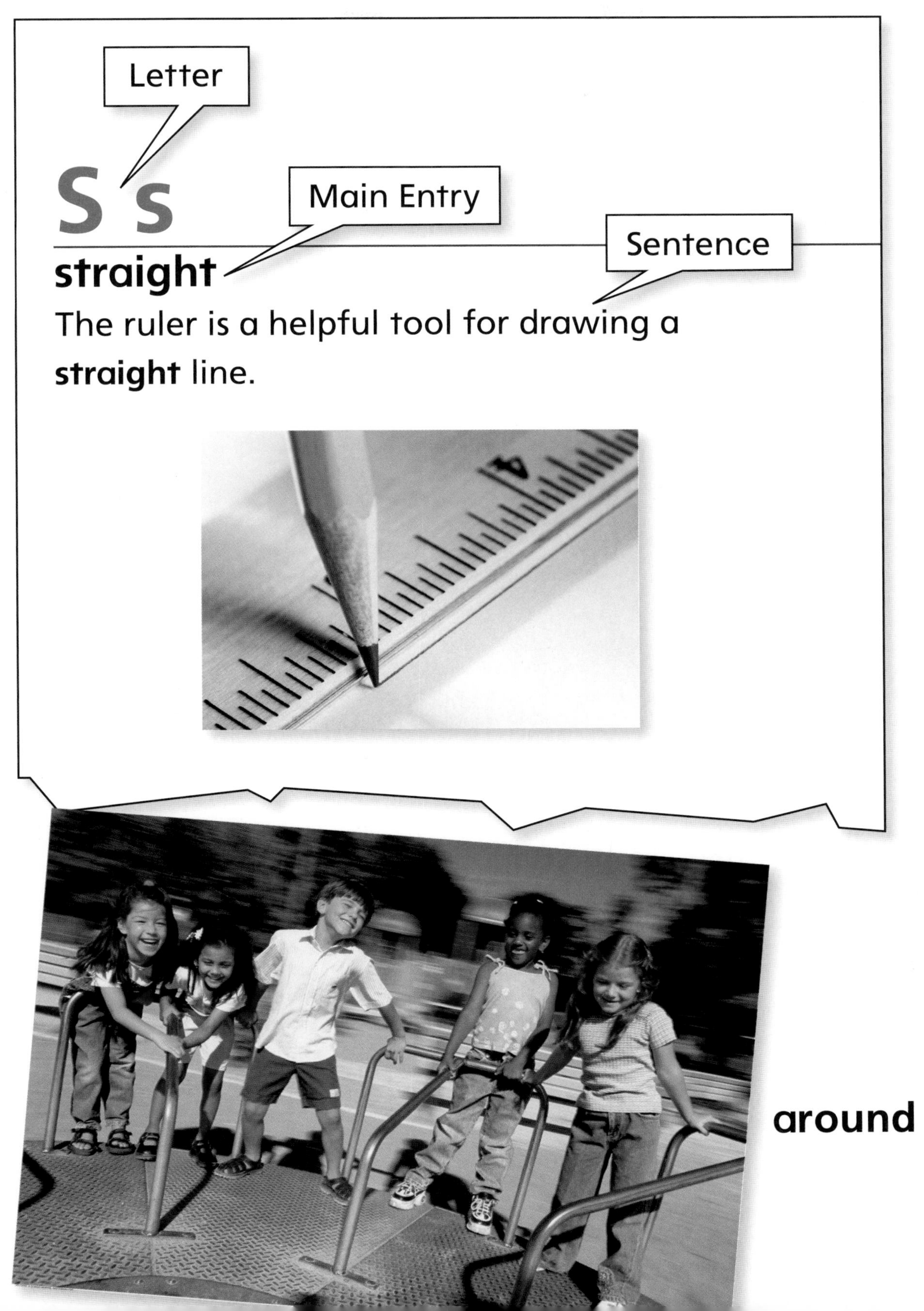

Aa

along

The boys hiked **along** a river.

always

Paul **always** arrives late.

around

We like to ride **around** and around.

artists

Artists are showing their paintings in the gym.

Bb

been

The boys were dirty because they had **been** playing in the mud.

before

Before he throws the ball, the player jumps as high as he can.

begin

When fall starts, leaves **begin** to pile up in the yard.

brought

Kit **brought** her little brother with her.

build

Beavers **build** dams in ponds and rivers.

Cc

cancel

If it rains, we'll **cancel** the picnic.

certain

Certain cats come when you call them.

clues

The **clues** helped Jim solve the mystery.

colors

The rainbow had many **colors**.

commands

Trained dogs learn to follow **commands**.

Dd

daydream

Try not to **daydream** in class.

Ee

early

Pete wakes us **early** in the morning.

errand

Tom ran an **errand** for his mom.

Ff

father

Jack and his **father** are cooking dinner.

firm

The teacher is **firm** about the rules.

four

There are **four** slices of bread left.

Gg

goes

A train **goes** fast.

gone

The pickles are all **gone**.

guide

The **guide** took our class through the museum.

Hh

harness

That **harness** is for the brown horse.

Ii

insects

All **insects** have six legs and three body parts.

instead

I chose the red shirt **instead** of the blue one.

interesting

I read an **interesting** book.

invisible

The brown lizard is almost **invisible** on the sand.

Ll

laugh

We **laugh** a lot when we are together.

love

I **love** my pet.

Mm

minutes

There are 60 **minutes** in an hour.

mother

My **mother** always braids my hair.

Nn

nothing

I bought **nothing** at the store.

Oo

only

There was **only** one pencil left.

ordinary
On an **ordinary** day, Maya plays outside after school.

protects
An umbrella **protects** me from the rain.

sculpture
The artist used clay to make a **sculpture**.

searching
I spent a long time **searching** for my sock.

senses

You use your five **senses** to taste, smell, see, hear, and touch.

straight

The ruler is a helpful tool for drawing a **straight** line.

suddenly

Suddenly the room got dark.

supposed

I am **supposed** to go to bed early.

Tt

thought

He **thought** hard when he took the test.

Acknowledgments

The publisher gratefully acknowledges permission to reprint the following copyrighted material:

"Dancing Paper" from *Confetti: Poems for Children* by Pat Mora. Text copyright © 1996 by Pat Mora. Reprinted with permission of Lee & Low Books, Inc.

Dot & Jabber and the Big Bug Mystery by Ellen Stoll Walsh. Text and illustrations copyright © 2003 by Ellen Stoll Walsh. Reprinted by permission of Harcourt, Inc.

Olivia by Ian Falconer. Copyright © 2000 by Ian Falconer. Reprinted by permission of Atheneum Books for Young Readers, an imprint of Simon & Schuster Children's Publishing Division.

Super Oscar by Oscar De La Hoya, illustrated by Lisa Kopelke. Text copyright © 2006 by Oscar De La Hoya. Illustrations copyright © 2006 by Lisa Kopelke. Used with permission of Simon & Schuster Books for Young Readers, an imprint of Simon & Schuster Children's Publishing Division.

Whistle for Willie by Ezra Jack Keats. Text and illustrations copyright © 1964 by Ezra Jack Keats. Reprinted by permission of the Penguin Group, a division of Penguin Putnam Books for Young Readers.

Book Cover, HOP JUMP by Ellen Stoll Walsh. Copyright © 1993 by Ellen Stoll Walsh. Reprinted by permission of Harcourt Brace & Company.

Book Cover, GOGGLES! by Ezra Jack Keats. Copyright © 1969 by Ezra Jack Keats. Reprinted by permission of Viking, an imprint of Penguin Putnam Books for Young Readers.

Book Cover, MOUSE PAINT by Ellen Stoll Walsh. Copyright © 1989 by Ellen Stoll Walsh. Reprinted by permission of Harcourt Brace & Company.

Book Cover, OLIVIA AND THE MISSING TOY by Ian Falconer. Copyright © 2003 by Ian Falconer. Reprinted by permission of Atheneum Books for Young Readers, an imprint of Simon & Schuster Children's Publishing Division.

Book Cover, OLIVIA SAVES THE CIRCUS by Ian Falconer. Copyright © 2001 by Ian Falconer. Reprinted by permission of Atheneum Books for Young Readers, an imprint of Simon & Schuster Children's Publishing Division.

ILLUSTRATIONS

Cover Illustration: Leland Klanderman

8–9: Tiphanie Beeke. 10–35: Ian Falconer. 36–39: Nancy Davis. 40: Ken Bowser. 44–45: Michael-Che Swisher. 46–75: Ezra Jack Keats. 100–101: Will Terry. 102–129: Ellen Stoll Walsh. 130–133: Susan Swan. 134: Rachel Geswaldo. 138–139: Holli Conger. 140–161: Lisa Kopelke. 164–165: Susan Swan. 162–163: Lisa Kopelke. 166: Jenny Vainisi. 168–169: Janee Trasler.

PHOTOGRAPHY

All Photographs are by Ken Cavanagh or Ken Karp for Macmillan/McGraw-Hill (MMH) except as noted below.

Inside front & back covers: Royalty-Free/CORBIS. v: Photodisc/Punchstock. 2-3: Jason Lindsey/Alamy. 3: Neil Beckerman/Getty Images. 4: Comstock Images. 5: George Tiedemann/CORBIS. 6-7: Jiang Jin/SuperStock. 34: Courtesy of Roddy McDowell. 37: Malcah Zeldis/Art Resource, NY. 38: (t) Art Resource, NY; (b) Erich Lessing/Art Resource, NY. 39: Victoria & Albert Museum, London/Art Resource, NY. 40: George Shelley/CORBIS. 41: Johner/Getty Images. 42-43: Jeff Cadge/Getty Images. 74: Courtesy of Ezra Jack Keats. 76: Digital Vision/Getty Images. 76-77: (b) Westend61/Alamy. 77: Paul Doyle/Alamy. 78: (l) Richard Sobol/Animals Animals; (r) Phanie/Photo Researchers. 78-79: (b) Westend61/Alamy. 79: tbkmedia.de/Alamy. 80: Stephen Simpson/Getty Images. 81: S.Meltzer/PhotoLink/Getty Images. 82-83: Photodisc/PunchStock. 84-85: Zephyr Picture/Index Stock. 85: Jose Luis Pelaez, Inc./CORBIS. 86: Tim Wimbourne/Reuters/Newscom. 88: (all photos) Janet Worne/Lexington Herald-Leader/KRT/Newscom. 89: (tl, cr) Burke/Triolo Productions/Getty Images; (tr) JUPITERIMAGES/ ABLESTOCK/Alamy; (cl) Royalty-Free/CORBIS; (b) Richard Smith/Masterfile. 90: (tl) AP-Wide World Photos; (tc) Stefan Sollfors/Alamy; (tcr) JUPITERIMAGES/Creatas/Alamy; (tr) Burke/Triolo Productions/Brand X Pictures/Getty Images; (cr) G.K. & Vikki Hart/Getty Images; (bl) Stefan Sollfors/Alamy; (b) JUPITERIMAGES/PHOTOS.COM/Alamy. 91: (tr) AP-Wide World Photos; (c) Stefan Sollfors/Alamy; (bl) Burke/Triolo Productions/Brand X Pictures/Getty Images; (bcl) Julie Toy/Getty Images; (bc) Maximilian Stock-StockFood Munich/Stockfood America; (br) G.K. & Vikki Hart/Getty Images. 92: Creatas/Jupiter Images. 92-93: Steve Craft/Masterfile. 93: (bl) Photolink/Getty Images; (br) William Fritsch/Brand X Pictures/Jupiter Images. 94: Richard Lord/The Image Works. 95: (cl) David Buffington/Getty Images; (c) Michael Newman/Photo Edit; (cr) AP Wide World Photos. 96: Digital Vision. 97: (t) Photo Link/Getty Images; (c) Bet Noire/Shutterstock; (b) Gabe Palmer/Alamy. 98-99: Nick Garbutt/Nature Picture Library. 128: Courtesy of Ellen Stoll Walsh. 130: (c) Burke/Triolo Productions/Brand X Pictures/Getty Images; (cr) Ingram Publishing/Alamy; (br) Photodisc/Getty Images. 131: (t) Charles Krebs/Getty Images; (tr) Ron Wu/Index Stock; (cr) Dynamic Graphics Group/Creatas/Alamy; (br) Bob London/CORBIS; (bl) Brian Hagiwara/Jupiter Images; (cl) Burke/Triolo Productions/Brand X Pictures/Getty Images. 132: (tl) Werner H. Müller/CORBIS; (c) Brian Hagiwara/Brand X/CORBIS. 133: (tr) Anthony Bannister; Gallo Images/CORBIS; (c) IT Stock Free/AGE Fotostock. 134: BananaStock/PunchStock. 135: Digital Archive Japan/PunchStock. 136-137: ColorBlind Images/Getty Images. 158: J.P. Yim/ZUMA/CORBIS. 166: Image Source/PunchStock. 167: Creatas/PunchStock. 170: (tl) E. R. Degginger/Photo Researchers; (br) Gail Shumway/Getty Images. 171: (t to b) DAVID M. DENNIS/Animals Animals; David Liebman © Pink Guppy; DAVID M. DENNIS/Animals Animals; Margarette Mead/Getty Images. 174: (cr) Burke/Triolo Productions/Brand X Pictures/Getty Images; (bl) Goodshoot/Fotosearch. 175: (t) Corbis/Superstock; (b) Rommel/Masterfile. 176: Rommel/Masterfile. 177: Photolink/Getty Images. 178: Goodshoot/Fotosearch. 179: Ariel Skelley/CORBIS. 180: (t) Photographer's Choice/Getty Images; (b) Burke/Triolo Productions/Brand X Pictures/Getty Images. 181: Peter Hince/Getty Images. 182: Royalty-Free/CORBIS. 183: Image Source/Jupiter Images. 184: Corbis/Superstock. CA Standards pages 1-4: Medioimages/PunchStock.

Reading/Language Arts
CA California Standards
Grade 1

READING

1.0 Word Analysis, Fluency, and Systematic Vocabulary Development
Students understand the basic features of reading. They select letter patterns and know how to translate them into spoken language by using phonics, syllabication, and word parts. They apply this knowledge to achieve fluent oral and silent reading.

Concepts About Print

1.1 Match oral words to printed words.

1.2 Identify the title and author of a reading selection.

1.3 Identify letters, words, and sentences.

Phonemic Awareness

1.4 Distinguish initial, medial, and final sounds in single-syllable words.

1.5 Distinguish long-and short-vowel sounds in orally stated single-syllable words (e.g., *bit/bite)*.

1.6 Create and state a series of rhyming words, including consonant blends.

1.7 Add, delete, or change target sounds to change words (e.g., change *cow* to *how; pan* to *an)*.

1.8 Blend two to four phonemes into recognizable words (e.g., */c/ a/ t/* = cat; */f/ l/ a/ t/* = flat).

1.9 Segment single-syllable words into their components (e.g., */c/ a/ t/* = cat; */s/ p/ l/ a/ t/* = splat; */r/ i/ ch/* = rich).

Decoding and Word Recognition

1.10 Generate the sounds from all the letters and letter patterns, including consonant blends and long-and short-vowel patterns (i.e., phonograms), and blend those sounds into recognizable words.

1.11 Read common, irregular sight words (e.g., *the, have, said, come, give, of)*.

1.12 Use knowledge of vowel digraphs and *r-* controlled letter-sound associations to read words.

1.13 Read compound words and contractions.

1.14 Read inflectional forms (e.g., *-s, -ed, -ing)* and root words (e.g., *look, looked, looking)*.

1.15 Read common word families (e.g., *-ite, -ate)*.

1.16 Read aloud with fluency in a manner that sounds like natural speech.

Vocabulary and Concept Development
1.17 Classify grade-appropriate categories of words (e.g., concrete collections of animals, foods, toys).
2.0 **Reading Comprehension** Students read and understand grade-level-appropriate material. They draw upon a variety of comprehension strategies as needed (e.g., generating and responding to essential questions, making predictions, comparing information from several sources). The selections in *Recommended Literature, Kindergarten Through Grade Twelve* illustrate the quality and complexity of the materials to be read by students. In addition to their regular school reading, by grade four, students read one-half million words annually, including a good representation of grade-level-appropriate narrative and expository text (e.g., classic and contemporary literature, magazines, newspapers, online information). In grade one, students begin to make progress toward this goal.
Structural Features of Informational Materials
2.1 Identify text that uses sequence or other logical order.
Comprehension and Analysis of Grade-Level-Appropriate Text
2.2 Respond to *who, what, when, where,* and *how* questions.
2.3 Follow one-step written instructions.
2.4 Use context to resolve ambiguities about word and sentence meanings.
2.5 Confirm predictions about what will happen next in a text by identifying key words (i.e., signpost words).
2.6 Relate prior knowledge to textual information.
2.7 Retell the central ideas of simple expository or narrative passages.
3.0 **Literary Response and Analysis** Students read and respond to a wide variety of significant works of children's literature. They distinguish between the structural features of the text and the literary terms or elements (e.g., theme, plot, setting, characters). The selections in *Recommended Literature, Kindergarten Through Grade Twelve* illustrate the quality and complexity of the materials to be read by students.
Narrative Analysis of Grade-Level-Appropriate Text
3.1 Identify and describe the elements of plot, setting, and character(s) in a story, as well as the story's beginning, middle, and ending.
3.2 Describe the roles of authors and illustrators and their contributions to print materials.
3.3 Recollect, talk, and write about books read during the school year.

WRITING

1.0 Writing Strategies Students write clear and coherent sentences and paragraphs that develop a central idea. Their writing shows they consider the audience and purpose. Students progress through the stages of the writing process (e.g., prewriting, drafting, revising, editing successive versions).

Organization and Focus

1.1 Select a focus when writing.

1.2 Use descriptive words when writing.

Penmanship

1.3 Print legibly and space letters, words, and sentences appropriately.

2.0 Writing Applications (Genres and Their Characteristics) Students write compositions that describe and explain familiar objects, events, and experiences. Student writing demonstrates a command of standard American English and the drafting, research, and organizational strategies outlined in Writing Standard 1.0.
Using the writing strategies of grade one outlined in Writing Standard 1.0, students:

2.1 Write brief narratives (e.g., fictional, autobiographical) describing an experience.

2.2 Write brief expository descriptions of a real object, person, place, or event, using sensory details.

WRITTEN AND ORAL ENGLISH LANGUAGE CONVENTIONS

The standards for written and oral English language conventions have been placed between those for writing and for listening and speaking because these conventions are essential to both sets of skills.

1.0 Written and Oral English Language Conventions Students write and speak with a command of standard English conventions appropriate to this grade level.

Sentence Structure

1.1 Write and speak in complete, coherent sentences.

Grammar

1.2 Identify and correctly use singular and plural nouns.

1.3 Identify and correctly use contractions (e.g., *isn't, aren't, can't, won't)* and singular possessive pronouns (e.g., *my/ mine, his/ her, hers, your/s)* in writing and speaking.

Punctuation	
1.4	Distinguish between declarative, exclamatory, and interrogative sentences.
1.5	Use a period, exclamation point, or question mark at the end of sentences.
1.6	Use knowledge of the basic rules of punctuation and capitalization when writing.
Capitalization	
1.7	Capitalize the first word of a sentence, names of people, and the pronoun *I*.
Spelling	
1.8	Spell three-and four-letter short-vowel words and grade-level-appropriate sight words correctly.

LISTENING AND SPEAKING

1.0 **Listening and Speaking Strategies** Students listen critically and respond appropriately to oral communication. They speak in a manner that guides the listener to understand important ideas by using proper phrasing, pitch, and modulation.

Comprehension	
1.1	Listen attentively.
1.2	Ask questions for clarification and understanding.
1.3	Give, restate, and follow simple two-step directions.
Organization and Delivery of Oral Communication	
1.4	Stay on the topic when speaking.
1.5	Use descriptive words when speaking about people, places, things, and events.

2.0 **Speaking Applications (Genres and Their Characteristics)** Students deliver brief recitations and oral presentations about familiar experiences or interests that are organized around a coherent thesis statement. Student speaking demonstrates a command of standard American English and the organizational and delivery strategies outlined in Listening and Speaking Standard 1.0.

Using the speaking strategies of grade one outlined in Listening and Speaking Standard 1.0, students:

2.1	Recite poems, rhymes, songs, and stories.
2.2	Retell stories using basic story grammar and relating the sequence of story events by answering *who, what, when, where, why,* and *how* questions.
2.3	Relate an important life event or personal experience in a simple sequence.
2.4	Provide descriptions with careful attention to sensory detail.